Introd
Patterns fo

by

Three Members of
the Church of England Liturgical Commission
concerning the Commission's Report *Patterns for Worship*
(Church House Publishing, 1989)

Trevor Lloyd
Archdeacon of Barnstaple

Jane Sinclair
Lecturer in Christian Worship, St. John's College, Nottingham

Michael Vasey
Lecturer, in Christian Worship, Cranmer Hall, Durham

GROVE BOOKS LIMITED
Bramcote Nottingham NG9 3DS

CONTENTS

THE COVER PICTURE

is by Jane Sinclair

First Impression January 1990
ISSN 0144-1728
ISBN 1 85174 134 8

1. HAVE THEY GONE MAD?

by Michael Vasey

30 November 1989 saw the publication of *Patterns for Worship*[1], the most substantial production so far from the Liturgical Commission appointed for the term of the 1985-1990 General Synod. Published as a Report for the General Synod with a Prefatory Note by the House of Bishops, it is due to be considered in a 'take note' debate in February 1990.

The format of *Patterns* is likely to confuse those who are at home with the orderly, linear style of official reports. It reads like the unfinished proofs of a resource book, or like a manual before the illustrations and colour-coded charts have been added. The publication of Series 3 Holy Communion in 1971 broke new ground in the typography and layout of liturgical texts.[2] *Lent, Holy Week, Easter* followed the example of other churches in prefacing the liturgical texts with concise pastoral introductions. (This was hardly conceivable where line-by-line revision was required for synodical authorization).[3] Had it been possible to issue a full-colour edition of *Patterns* we might have been faced with colours and illustrations being subject to synodical revision! To understand the published Report readers need to abandon any notion of starting at the beginning and to don an imaginary pair of 3-D spectacles. Six sample service cards from the Report with colour and illustrations have been published as GS Misc. 328.

Of the 296 pages of the Report, 156 are devoted to resources sections of liturgical texts (pp.107-263)[4] and 75 to sample congregational service cards (pp.31-106). Much of this material can already be lawfully used under certain circumstances. The Report proposes two new rites for authorization. First, a more flexible form of Bible service that would become a lawful alternative to the Sunday Offices of the BCP and ASB, *Form of Service for Morning or Evening Prayer: The Service of the Word* (pp.16-17). Secondly, a more flexible form of the eucharist, *Form of Service for the Holy Communion, Rite C* (pp.18-20). Together they occupy only five pages. Each one indicates what may or must be present in the rite and when only authorized texts may be used. They are not intended for direct and unembellished liturgical use but provide the legal bases that must be agreed by Synod and parish before the more flexible forms they permit may be adopted.

[1] GS898, CHP.

[2] R. C. D. Jasper *The Development of the Anglican Liturgy 1662-1980* (SPCK, 1989) pp.312-313.

[3] As the services were deemed not alternative to those in the BCP full synodical approval was not required. They were 'commended' by the House of Bishops and are used under the authority of Canons B4 and B5.

[4] It does not help that the monochrome coding system for the Resources Sections is hidden on p.292.

The Report includes four different forms of guidance for this material:

1 *Introduction* (pp.1-15). This sets out the thinking behind the new forms. This includes a brief introduction to the eucharistic prayers. (Fuller comment by two members of the Commission, Bryan Spinks and Kenneth Stevenson, has been published, 'with the goodwill of the Commission as a whole', as GS Misc. 335).[1]

2. *Instructions* (pp. 21-29). These give guidance on how the services are to be put together. They refer to structure, content and general approach.

3. *The Commentary* (pp.264-286). Still incomplete, this aims to provide guidance on all the main elements in the services. 'We decided the most digestible and least legalistic way of doing it would be to tell stories. So here you have the stories of four entirely imaginery churches, told in sections that correspond with the Resources Sections'. (p.264)

4. *Legal and Doctrinal matters* (pp.287-291). Two Appendices deal with questions of common prayer, law and doctrine.[2]

The arrival on the scene of liturgical proposals on this scale is likely to prove a nasty shock to those who endured the many years of synodical debate that gave rise to the ASB 1980 and thought that liturgical stability would now settle on the church for at least a generation. In his first Presidential Address to General Synod on 8 July 1980 Robert Runcie declared with obvious relief, 'We stand at a point where the heroic age of constitutional and liturgical change is over'. In words that echoed those with which John Habgood had commended the ASB a year before the Archbishop said, 'I hope it will be easier once again to have a Prayer Book in the home and bring it to church. I hope that a varied and balanced teaching ministry may be built upon our Books, both of which reflect a worldwide Anglican face'.[3]

However understandable such a feeling may be, the arrival of *Patterns* should not take people by surprise. There have been many pointers towards a development in this direction. Furthermore many of the fears that some may have—of wearisome synodical process, or of constant change producing confusion rather than a deeper awareness of God—are shared by the Commission and addressed in the Report.

Pastoral need

Two of the great pastoral Church of England Reports of the 1980s, *Faith in the City* and *Children in the Way,* have criticized the inadequacy of the current worship position and made recommendations in the direction

[1] The prefatory note states,'These essays . . . remain, however the personal compositions of the two authors, and the views expressed are not necessarily the corporate views of the Commission'.

[2] See also chapter 3 below.

[3] *GS Proceedings* 1980 p.446 cf. 1979 p.684.

taken by *Patterns for Worship.*[1] Many of *Faith in the City's* comments are echoed in *Patterns:*

> '[Worship] will therefore reflect a universality of form with local variations, allowing significant space for worship that is genuinely local.
>
> '... more concrete and tangible rather than abstract and theoretical ...
>
> 'Is the worship lively and participatory? Does it evoke a sense of God while showing a concern for the real things in people's lives? ...
>
> 'Worship is about good dreams: it needs to hold them alongside what is sometimes a very harsh reality.
>
> 'We have heard calls for short functional service books or cards, prepared by people who always ask "if all the words are really necessary".'

Children in the Way recommends that the 'Liturgical Commission examine the need for new liturgies to serve all-age worship, and in particular for a form of Eucharist suitable for when children are present'.

Pressure for additional provision has not been limited to official reports. There have been repeated requests for the authorization of eucharistic prayers 'for use with children' (strange while the Knaresborough Report gathers dust![2]). The House of Laity passed a motion asking for an adequate provision of non-eucharistic as well as eucharistic services.

Most significant of all is the continuing phenomenon of the Family Service. An excellent and detailed report from the Diocese of Chelmsford notes that these occur in nearly 50% of parishes: in two-thirds of these attendance was higher than at other times. The report notes that Family Services are more than a bridge into normal church life: 'they have become another strand of Anglican worship'.[3] Both *Children in the Way* and *Patterns* discuss the various pitfalls to which this tradition is prone and are strongly critical of the title 'family Service'.[4]

In August 1986 Nigel McCulloch, Bishop of Taunton, renewed the call for these to be regularized. 'Otherwise we will continue to have this odd situation: that the service which locals regard as the main act of worship in their parish church (because it is always the best attended) is neither in its content nor its conducting an authorized service of the Church of England'.[5]

[1] *Faith in the City* (CHP 1985) pp.134-137, (cf. John Bentham *Worship in the City* (Grove Worship Series 95, 1986)); *Children in the Way* (National Society/CHP 1988) pp.49-53.

[2] The 'Knaresborough Report' is the Report of the working party chaired by the then Bishop of Knaresborough, *Communion before Confirmation?* (Church House Publishing, 1985). It was debated once in Synod in November 1985 and has since rested with the House of Bishops.

[3] *For the Family* (Diocese of Chelmsford 1987) p.4.

[4] *Children in the Way* pp.50-52; pp.30-33. *Patterns* pp.2-5.

[5] *Bath and Wells Diocesan News* August 1986. See also *Church Times* 25.7.86.

An old question

The impression is often given that 'Family Services' (for want of a better word!) are not lawful, or again that the question of the authorization of more flexible and popular forms of worship has only arisen recently. Neither of these is correct.

Canon B5.2 provides that 'the minister may on occasions for which there is no provision . . . use forms of service considered suitable by him for those occasions'. Canon B5.3 requires that such a service shall be 'reverent and seemly and shall be neither contrary to, nor indicative of any departure from, the doctrine of the Church of England in any essential matter'. If any illegality exists it will lie in not seeking the bishop's permission to dispense with the reading of Morning Prayer (Canon B11.2) or in not celebrating the Holy Communion on a Sunday (Canon B14).

The precise wording of Canon B5.2 dates from 1975 but some such provision has existed since the 1872 Shortened Services Act. This allowed a minister to compose a service for special occasions (from the Bible and the Prayer Book and with episcopal approval) and to hold a 'third Service' on a Sunday (using any part of the Prayer Book apart from the Communion Service).[1]

The term 'Family Service' may be comparatively recent but for more than a century there have been voices proclaiming the inadequacy of the official provisions. The chaplains in the First World War discovered:

> 'Hardly a soldier carries a Prayer Book, because there is little in it he can use . . . We never guessed of old how removed it was from common wants; nor how intellectual are its prayers and forms of devotion. Its climate to the simple, ardent Christian is often ice. The warm romance of man's pilgrimage to God is absent from it'.[2]

These complaints fuelled the pressure for Prayer Book revision after the War but seem to have had no impact on the 1928 Prayer Book.

In 1967 the Liturgical Commission published a book *Family and Evangelistic Services* written by John Wilkinson. It is surprising how little it has dated. Its basic treatment of service structure and approach anticipates *Patterns* (although it still thinks of these services as a bridge to 'normal' Anglican worship). This similarity extends to matters of detail.[3] This book was followed by a 'five page typewritten' report arguing that 'the needs of the people who attended such services . . . should be met . . . by providing a selection of suitable structures and a wide choice of material'.[4] This was accepted by the Bishops, commended to the dioceses and lost without trace!

[1] R. C. D. Jasper p.57.
[2] E. Milner-White in *The Church in the Furnace* ed. F. C. MacNutt, 1917 pp.184-185.
[3] e.g. Creeds (p.23); and the collection (p.25), 'it should be treated as part of the Prayers: an expression in action of the prayer of self-dedication'.
[3] R. C. D. Jasper p.275.

Patterns for Worship has its official origin in a paper of the Standing Committee *The Worship of the Church*[1] debated in Synod in November 1985 and in a decision of the House of Bishops of June 1986.[2] The debate in Synod often focused on whether, and how soon, the ASB should be replaced. This may turn out to be the wrong question. The prior question is, What provision is to be made for more popular forms of worship? On the important issue of the time needed for people to assimilate new forms of worship, one speaker pleaded for the trust 'to stand still and do nothing'. The point is surely sound as a comment on local practice; *St. David's* in the Commentary provides hilarious vignettes of insensitive change.[3] Brian Brindley's riposte was, 'she was really asking us only to have only one play in our repertoire and to keep on performing it'![4]

As *Patterns* goes to Synod it is worth asking why similar proposals have been so effectively ignored in the past. The question is an important and uncomfortable one for the Church of England. The answer is probably more complex thaqn the common human failings of spiritual blindness and failure of imagination. One element must be a sense of inadequacy in the face of the demands these services make on the whole church as well as on the clergy.

Two others are worth a mention at this point. Anglican tradition has often given the impression that the only serious or worthy forms of non-eucharistic Sunday worship are the Office or the Ante-Communion. In a short but helpful discussion *Patterns* shows that this is too simple an account of liturgical history; the Service of the Word legitimately takes a variety of forms (pp.6-11).

A second element is a failure to understand the varied social function of books.[5] Anglican tradition has conflated the different functions of theological witness, liturgical manual and devotional primer. Even the ASB lacks plausibility as a devotional primer; it lacks a catechism or prayers at death but includes the blessing of an abbot! *Patterns* stands clearly in the tradition of the liturgical manual.

Authorization

Much of the material in *Patterns* can already be used under the provisions of Canon B5. Section 7 (p.vii) and section 2 (pp.287/8) indicate the course likely to follow a positive debate in Synod. The legal outlines for the Service of the Word and Rite C, together with the alternative penitential material, eucharistic prayers and possibly the affirmations of faith would require Synodical approval. The rest would be revised and then commended by the House of Bishops in the same way as *Lent, Holy Week, Easter.*

[1] GS698. Paragraph 5 makes it clear that this was an amended version of a report from the Litugical Commission. The Standing Committee, unlike the Liturgical Commission, wished to extend the authorization of the ASB to 2000. GS698 speaks of a 'directory' (para.40), a term later dropped because of its associations with the Westminster Directory, and with the telephone directory!

[2] Quoted in *Patterns* p.v.

[3] e.g. p.284.

[4] *GS Proceedings* 1985 pp.1053, 1060.

[5] Cf. Colin Buchanan, Trevor Lloyd, Michael Vasey (eds.) *Anglican Worship Today* (Collins, 1980) pp.47-48, 38-40. Michael Vasey *Reading the Bible at the Eucharist* (Grove Worship Series no. 94, 1986) pp.7-9.

2. NEW FREEDOM, NEW RESOURCES

by Jane Sinclair

The General Synod edition of *Patterns for Worship* (GS 898) appears at first sight to be a rather densely packed book, full of liturgical texts and difficult to find one's way around. It is well worth persevering! Contained within its covers are a wide range of provisions which will act as stimuli to and guidelines for the development of Church of England worship at the end of the twentieth century.

This chapter explores some of the new freedoms which *Patterns for Worship* brings to worship structures and content in the Church of England. But the exploration can only be made in a limited way in written form: it is inherent in the nature of *Patterns for Worship* that much of the initiative for developing the use of its material appropriate to a congregation must come from that congregation and its minister(s). To rework an analogy once used of the Alternative Service Book: if the ASB may be represented as a packet of 'frozen peas' (prepared at the factory, but needed to be heated through and served locally in order to be of any use!), then *Patterns for Worship* may be represented as a good recipe book and a hamper of choice ingredients. It will need well-informed local ministers and leaders of worship to make good use of the opportunities which it has to offter.

Opportunities for reshaping worship

In many respects pages 16-29 of *Patterns for Worship* contain the most innovative material in the book. It is here that the provisions for the structuring of services of the Word and the Holy communion are to be found.

It is commonplace that Anglicans are known as people of 'a book', usually taken to refer to the Alternative Service Book.[1] Within these books are contained full orders of service for various regular and special occasions. The ASB is notable in comparison to the BCP for the relative elasticity of its rubrics: for example, in Rite A at the introduction of the Peace the president 'says either of the following or other suitable words'. Whilst Anglicans may still hold a service book in their hands in order to follow the service, there is considerable freedom to vary the words from those printed in the book. Likewise, the structure of services may be varied according to options given within ASB services. The principle of some considerable degree of variation in forms of worship is already well established in Anglican practice, in England and in Anglican churches overseas.[2]

[1] This phrase originates in the days of the BCP only. However, it was part of the argument deployed to make the case in the 1970s for a large single-volume hardback ASB. Whether the concept of everyone having and using her or his own book has survived till the 1990s is open to question.

[2] For example, *A New Zealand Prayer Book* (1989); *The Book of Alternative Services* (1985) of the Anglican Church of Canada; *The Book of Common Prayer* (1979) of the Episcopal Church of the United States of America.

Patterns for Worship returns to the principles upon which these acknowledged freedoms rest and develops their application to forms of worship in the Church of England. These may be summarized:

1. A clear structure for any act of worship is essential. New freedoms in worship cannot be explored if worshippers are insecure about how they are being enabled to pray, praise, confess, and thank God. The main components of any act of worship ought therefore to stand out so that worshippers can see the shape, development and 'climax' of the service. New freedoms do not mean that 'anything goes'.
2. In the Introduction to *Patterns for Worship,* a strong case is argued for the interchangeability of the ante-communion (synaxis) and a service of the Word (a non-eucharistic Sunday service such as Morning or Evening Prayer). This may have helpful and creative implications for those churches which are developing all-age worship: it will be possible to have a common pattern of service of the Word whether as part of a eucharist or standing in its own right on another occasion. *Patterns for Worship* goes so far as to give a broad hint (p.8) that some churches may find it helpful to develop a pattern which involves a definite break (perhaps with tea and coffee) between the 'word' and 'sacrament' components of the Sunday Holy Communion in order to allow those who do not or cannot stay for communion to leave without embarrassment.
3. Any service—be it a service of the Word or the Holy Communion—must be balanced in its content. No service should simply contain praise and no teaching, or teaching but no prayer. If, in the words of 1 Corinthians 14.26, worship is to be 'edifying' for worshippers it needs to be well structured and of balanced content.

The Instructions for the Service of the Word develop this last point in detail. In any service of the Word (whether on its own, or leading into the Holy Communion) there should be a balance between four main ingredients:

- **Word** (reading(s) from scripture; sermon, instruction, address or their equivalent; sentences)
- **Prayer** (intercession; collect(s) and other forms of prayer; thanksgiving; etc.)
- **Praise** (psalms; hymns; songs and canticles; acclamations; etc.)
- **Action** (this is of a different order to the first three and may be used in conjunction with any of them, or in its own right. For example, the Peace; changes of posture during worship; processions; drama; dance).

The order in which these ingredients come is to be decided locally by the minister in consultation with the PCC (or, more usually, a worship group responsible to the PCC). Whilst *Patterns for Worship* gives several examples of the variety of order in which these ingredients may come (see pp.21-24 and the sample services on pp.32-105), it deliberately does not specify any mandatory order. In the spirit of the report *Faith in the City*[1], *Patterns* is designed to enable local priorities to shape local worship.

[1] *Faith in the City,* the report of the Archbishop's Commission on Urban Priority Areas, (Church House Publishing, London, 1985) pp.134-135.

If the order for the service of the Word (and therefore the first part of the Communion service) is therefore very flexible, there are nonetheless some limits drawn on its content in order to guard the orthodoxy and catholicity of a local congregation's worship. The Introduction to *Patterns for Worship* (pp.5-6) lists what the Liturgical Commission sees as marks 'which should be safeguarded for those who wish to stand in recognizable continuity with historic Anglican tradition'. These are:

- a recognizable structure for worship
- an emphasis on reading the word and on using psalms
- liturgical words repeated by the congregation, some of which, like the creed, would be known by heart
- using a collect, the Lord's Prayer, and some responsive forms of prayer
- a recognition of the centrality of the Eucharist
- a concern for form, dignity, and economy of words.

The Outline Instructions for the Service of the Word and for the Holy Communion Rite C demonstrate clearly what minimum elements are mandatory for inclusion within a *Patterns for Worship* service, however the service is structured. It is worth noting that within these mandatory elements there are some further restrictions on texts which have proved to be theologically sensitive in the past. Only fully authorized confessions, absolutions, creeds/affirmations of faith, eucharistic prayers and blessings may be used. Full details are given on pages 16-20 of *Patterns for Worship.*

Opportunities for reading the Bible afresh

Since the publication of the ASB there have been many calls for revision of the two year Sunday eucharistic lectionary.[1] In part, these calls are based on the experience of using a thematic lectionary over the course of a decade. Although there is provision for three readings at every Sunday service of Holy Communion, there is still a reluctance to use the Old Testament reading, even in the Advent to Christmas period when it is the controlling reading. Moreover, the thematic concerns informing the choice of readings Sunday by Sunday means that there is little chance to study any one book of the Bible in depth over a number of weeks with a Sunday congregation. The result is that many churches do not use the current lectionary provision. Readings are omitted or changed to fit the service theme. At worst, this results in a narrower overall diet of scripture, possible dictated by the particular interests of the minister.

Not only the content of the ASB lectionary has been criticized. In an age well accustomed to professional presentation on the television and in the press, the shoddy reading and presentation of scripture in some churches stands out as a glaring disservice to the word of God. Readers need to be trained to read aloud in public, and if necessary need to be taught how to use a microphone. Congregations need to have their expectations raised: if this is the word of God which we are hearing, let's expect to hear God speaking to us through it.

[1] A recently published example is Martin Dudley's essay on 'The Lectionary' from M. Perham (ed.) *Towards Liturgy 2000* (SPCK/Alcuin, 1989) pp.35-42.

Patterns for Worship offers two approaches to these problems:

1 Congregations need to be helped to rediscover the sheer excitement of reading the scriptures in worship. The Introduction to *Patterns for Worship* (pp.9-10) underlines the point that the scriptures are not simply given to us as a means for teaching: they are normative to and determinative of Christian faith and experience. They form the people of God as the people of God.
Suggestions for how congregations might be encouraged in this way are contained in the Commentary section of the report (pp.280-282). Important amongst them are the increased use of meditative silence (not simply imposed on a congregation, but introduced with teaching on how to use such silence); the use of acclamations or the verses of a psalm to express response to a reading; the use of drama, dance, choral reading, or other forms of presentation. In short, the report encourages the use of imagination in presenting the Bible so that its stories and teaching may be heard afresh in our churches.

2 Further and more imaginative lectionary provision should be made by the Church of England. In particular, the value of story should be reappropriated. *Patterns of Worship* argues strongly for the enrichment of the ASB lectionary provision, currently lacking much extended narrative material. It should be possible to experiment with a 'closed season' around the main festivals of the Church's year (Advent/Christmas, Lent/Easter, Pentecost), when a restricted seasonal lectionary should be mandatory for the whole Church. For the rest of the year, however, an 'open season' might be accommodated with several different lectionary options, one of which would consist of series of readings from major biblical narratives.
Examples of this approach are given on pages 127-130 of *Patterns for Worship.* The sample 'narrative' lections are designed in units of five or six weeks, suitable for family services and for adult worship.[1]

Designing 'open' and 'closed' lectionary seasons may seem novel to some ears, but it does have precedent. Lectionaries developed only gradually in the early church. As late as the end of the fourth century, Augustine comments that lections may be chosen at the discretion of the preacher if he so wishes. Since the Reformation, Anglicans themselves have been divided over the proper use of lectionaries. The advantage of the proposals made in *Patterns for Worship* is that they take seriously the needs of the local congregation, without losing the central importance of the major Christological feasts which unite the church in common celebration.

All-age worship: opportunities for children and adults

Patterns for Worship is designed to be used by all those who come to worship in the Church of England, no matter what their age. It is not a book solely for children, nor solely for adults: its provisions are offered for the use throughout the Church of England.

[1] The examples given include stories from the Jacob cycle (Genesis 25-33) and the Joseph cycle (Genesis 37-47). Thematic story approaches are given from the Gospels ('People Jesus met' and 'Time for a feast'). Note 6 on page 128 also provides for churches to design their own reading scheme for a limited period of the year in 'ordinary time'. on similar principles. Guidelines are offered on how such a course of readings might be designed in a balanced way.

This is an important principle to maintain, given the calls made in the *Faith in the City* report[1] and the report *Children in the Way*[2] for worship to be designed with the needs of particular user groups in mind. The Liturgical Commission has been well aware of the recommendations of official Church reports in these areas, but has deliberately set out to make provisions which in principle might be adapted to a rural church with few children present as much as to an inner urban church where 60% of the congregation may be under 16.

This having been said, there are various aspects in which *Patterns for Worship* may prove to be an enormous advantage to churches seeking to develop worship in mixed congregations of adults and children.

The four new proposed eucharistic prayers vary widely in style, theological emphases and in length; but all are considerably more responsive than those in the ASB or BCP. Where they are new, the responses may be easily learnt by heart. Eucharistic prayer D contains the Rite A responses, but within a much briefer presbyterial monologue. The Preface to Eucharistic prayer D may itself come from the 'Thanksgiving' section of the Resources material of *Patterns for Worship.* There are many opportunities here for using a Thanksgiving as part of a family service of the Word on one Sunday, and as a eucharistic preface on another Sunday.

The imaginative use of options for structure and content in worship given in *Patterns for Worship* cought to enable the development of all-age worship patterns which avoid the current tendency in many churches to settle either into a truncated form of ASB Morning Prayer, or into a mish-mash of readings, choruses and prayers. *Patterns for Worship* does not give a 'Family Worship' pattern for use in all churches, but the sample service cards do give worked examples of a variety of eucharistic and non-eucharistic services which may be suitable for use on different occasions. A useful checklist of Guidelines for use when preparing services from *Patterns for Worship* is also given on pages 25-26 of the report.

The language of the material in the Resources section shows evidence of having been influenced by pleas for language to be couched in graphic and narrative terms, rather than in the abstract language favoured in much of the ASB. For example, of the proposed confessions, one is based on the parable of the Prodigal Son, and another on Hosea 6:

> Lord our God,
> in our sin we have avoided your call.
> Our love for you is like the mist,
> disappearing in the heat of the sun . . .[3]

When members of the Liturgical Commission took these and other texts to a variety of urban parishes for trial use during 1988, the language of such texts was commented on with appreciation by children and adults alike.

[1] *Faith in the City,* p.135.
[2] *Children in the Way,* a report from the General Synod Board of Education (Church House Publishing, London, 1988) pp.49-52.
[3] *Patterns for Worship,* p.122, no. 16 2.9.

New opportunities . . . the end or the beginning?

Patterns for Worship is innovative for the Church of England in its style and in the forms in which its provisions are cast. In its concern to take seriously the urgent calls for liturgical sensitivity to the needs of widely differing congregations, *Patterns for Worship* poses questions about present suitability of forms of service which are not especially geared to local needs. The search has been to enable churches in rural, urban and suburban England to participate in the catholicity of the church's worship whilst expressing that worship in ways which are true to local cultures. It is doubtful whether that search has been completed with the publication of *Patterns for Worship.* Its use in the coming years should give further indications as to how the Church of England ought to approach the task of revising the ASB, or writing its successor, for the year 2000.

3. LIVING WITH FREEDOM

by Michael Vasey

What will change if Synod approves *Patterns for Worship* and authorizes *The Service of the Word* and *Rite C* for Parish use? Perhaps very little. 'Family' Services are already lawful and a good part of the material in *Patterns* can be used without authorization. Much of what it envisages takes place already without regard for such questions. But the new freedoms are a startling departure for a church which has thought it important to fix the rules and texts of its worship with great precision.

Freedom can be a heady brew as the political events of the last decade have demonstrated. New freedom in worship will leave some excited and others fearful. The first priority will be to work from a Christian understanding of freedom. Perhaps the classic New Testament treatment of freedom is Galatians 5. Some of St. Paul's themes are well expressed by ARCIC II:

> 'In restoring us to his likeness, God confers freedom on fallen humanity. This is not the natural freedom to choose between alternatives, but the freedom to do his will . . . We are freed and enabled to keep the commandments of God by the power of the Holy Spirit, to live faithfully as God's people and to grow in love within the discipline of the community, bringing forth the fruit of the Spirit. Our liberation commits us to an order of social existence in which the individual finds fulfilment in relationship with others. Thus freedom in Christ does not imply an isolated life, but rather one lived in a community governed by mutual obligations.[1]

How is the new freedom represented by *Patterns* to be evaluated?

What are its benefits?

Much of the rest of this booklet is devoted to the good things in *Patterns.* There is plenty of evidence that we need the flexibility and enrichment that it offers.

What are its dangers?

Anglicans have much to thank God for in their tradition of ordered worship. As the *Guidelines* to the Ecumenical Canons put it:

> 'The Church of England values the extensive use of agreed forms for a number of reasons: it preserves unity; it sustains theological orthodoxy and fullness; it helps congregational participation; it enables the wider Church as well as both minister and congregation to be confident about the content of significant prayers'.[2]

Many of these benefits may be put at risk by the new freedom envisaged in *Patterns.* The most obvious danger is sloppy, quirky worship, theologically thin or idiosyncratic, the product of ill-informed or undisciplined clerical whim. More long-term is the danger that people will lose the sense of unity that is sustained by common liturgical forms.

[1] *Salvation and the Church* (CTS/CHP, 1987) para. 19, 20.
[2] General Synod, 1989 Edition, p.22.

Another long-term danger is a gradual drift to sentimental worship devoid of strong doctrinal content. One of the important contributions of the Oxford Movement was a sense of confidence in the strong affirmations of the liturgy and the creeds. (Dropping the Apostles' Creed at the baptismal affirmation of faith in Series 2 and the ASB may already be an example of this drift). There is sensitivity to this issue in the Resources Section on Affirmations of Faith (p.131).

Fear is a bad teacher. These dangers are best avoided by positive action, which is why *Patterns* devotes so much attention to different forms of user-friendly guidance.

What are its limits?

The requirements set out in *The Service of the Word* and *Rite C,* and the rules about authorization etc. in Appendix 1 and 2, are not to be seen as a limitation on the freedomn of Christian worship but as its protection. They exist to ensure that worship reaches out towards God's fullness and builds up the church.

If this sounds pious it may indicate that we need as a church to move to a more theological and pastoral understanding of church law. Our current understanding is too shaped by a civic and individualist tradition of law. The question needs to be less, 'What am I now allowed to do?' as if a new sphere of private freedom has been opened up, and more, 'What norm does the church set before us as we try to serve God in this place?'.

1. Content

The Service of the Word. There is an interesting mix here of 'usually', 'normally', 'may', 'must' etc. It looks as if the term 'authorized' is in danger of being used to cover material that will only be 'commended'—a recipe for confusion? The only required texts are a confession and absolution, Praise responses, the Lord's Prayer and two approved collects. Two scripture readings are preferred to one. There is no requirement to use an authorized lectionary. It is perhaps unfortunate that there is no reference to the guidance on choosing readings in the Resources Section.[1] Only agreed forms of penitence, praise responses, affirmation of faith, and ending are to be used.

The ante-communion of *Rite C* can come from Morning or Evening Prayer, Rite A, *The Service of the Word* or the alternative set out as part of *Rite C.* This last requires at least two readings ('one of which shall be a Gospel'). In the eucharistic section only agreed texts may be used for the Eucharistic Prayer, the Fraction, the Blessing and Dismissal. (Are the words of distribution a deliberate omission?).

2. Leaders

The Service of the Word uses the term 'minister'. If it were authorized as an alternative form of Morning and Evening Prayer, such a service might fall under Canon B11, and leadership would be limited to clergy, 'readers and such other lay persons as may be authorized by the bishop of the diocese'.

[1] Para 6, p.128.

Rite C has no equivalent to Note 2 of Rite A. The President says the collect, the Eucharistic Prayer, the invitation to Communion, the Blessing and (by inference from a cross-reference to Rite A) the Dismissal.

3. Doctrine

The freedom in *Patterns* will put new responsibilities in the matter of doctrine on worship leaders, both ordained and lay. These must be understood and grasped if partiality and disunity are to be avoided. (Like other aspects of *Patterns* this may imply training).

Both *The Service of the Word* and *Rite C* print an opening Note:

> 'All vaiations of this form of service, and all forms used as part of it shall be neither contrary to, not indicative of any departure from, the doctrine of the Church of England in any essential matter'.

This reflects the important limit on the minister's discretion in Canon B5.4. Appendix 2 MATTERS OF DOCTRINE[1] amplifies this carefully with reference to scripture and tradition. In particular it says, 'Where, in controversial matters, General Synod has taken care not to depart from the teaching or usage found in [the 39 Articles and the Book of Coomon Prayer], this should be respected'.

Thus the eucharistic prayers in *Patterns* respect the way in which the controversial anamnesis paragraph was handled in the ASB although they go well beyond mere imitation.[2] (The ASB prayers are sometimes presented as mere compromise. It would be more just to see a principle of *restraint* operating; not departing from scripture or Church of England tradition in matters of controversy).[3]

The words 'in any essential matter' derive from the Worship and Doctrine Measure 1974. This measure requires that Synod be satisfied that any form of service it approves meets the same condition. Paradoxically this means that *Rite C* will need to be scrutized carefully as its Synodical approval will endorse any doctrinal innovations.[4]

4. Authorization

Two points need to be noted here.

(a) The results of Synod authorizing *The Service of the Word* according to the full liturgical procedure (as is proposed)[5] will need to be examined

[1] This is reproduced from *Ecumenical Relations* p.32. This Code of Practice also includes 'Commentary and Guidelines on Liturgical Matters' which breaks new ground in giving an official account of some sensitive areas. It could be useful as a training resource.

[2] By an oversight there is an ambiguity in the anamnesis of Echaristic Prayer D, (p.250). 'Remember' could be indicative or imperative. The addition of 'with hope' would remove the ambiguity and add an eschatological note.

[3] R. C. D. Jasper *Development* pp.253ff; 309ff; 351ff. C. O. Buchanan *Liturgy for Communion* (Grove Books, 1979) p.6, *passim.*

[4] Cf. the controversial ruling of Chancellor Garth Moore that a rubric in Series 2 had legalized reservation. (see C. O. Buchanan *Recent Liturgical Revision in the Church of England* p.30, and *Liturgy for Communion* p.19; *The Alternative Service Book 1980: A Commentary by the Liturgical Commission* p.79).

[5] p.287.

carefully. Strictly it would mean that this service is now available as an alternative Morning and Evening Prayer. However, it is likely to be understood as bringing all Sunday 'Family' Services under church regulation. The requirements of *The Service of the Word* are drawn sufficiently broadly that well-designed services will have nothing to fear. But, as indicated above, it would have implications as to the leadership of these services. The restrictions on Canon B11.4 could be softened by inserting an opening note:

> 'Where it is wished to invite someone without the bishop's licence to lead or preach on a regular basis the bishop's written approval must be obtained'.

(b) According to the 1974 Worship and Doctrine Measure (and Canon B3) the agreement of the PCC will be required before *The Service of the Word* or *Rite C* can be used. (The actual wording implied active partnership in making this decision).

As the law now stands, once a particular order of service is agreed the minister alone is responsible for deciding between the different options in the service.[1] This may seem odd. For historical reasons our tradition of church law is dominated by two figures, the sovereign and the incumbent. Two principles lie behind this: orthodoxy and unity require uniform rites that are determined nationally; the parish incumbent must be defended against local or ecclesiastical pressure to compromise the gospel.[2] The inadequacy of this tradition for modern pastoral demands should be obvious. The ASB goes a long way towards allowing parts of the service to be determined locally.

The freedom in *Patterns* makes it undesirable that the PCC should have no say as to which options are used. *Patterns* advises (pp.289/290) that the PCC should agree on:

(i) the frequency of the service;
(ii) any limitations on contents;
(iii) how long it will be used and when it will be reviewed.

These could be given the force of law by being included in opening notes to the service. They could be phrased to suggest the formation of a worship team recognized by the PCC. It might also be good to include a note that incumbent and others should seek advice and training from the diocesan liturgical group.

What are its consequences?

1. Common Prayer

The understandable concern that greater freedom will undermine the valued tradition of 'Common Prayer' is given extended consideration in *Patterns.*[3] A number of different ideals lie behind this term. Each has dif-

[1] *The Opinions of the Legal Advisory Commission* (Sixth Edition) p.138.
[2] For the careful limitation in modern times of the bishop's role in matters liturgical see C. O. Buchanan *Recent Liturgical Revision* pp.4-7; chapter by H. R. M. Craig in *Towards a Modern Prayer Book* ed. R. T. Beckwith (Marcham, 1966) pp.26-7.
[3] pp.5-6; pp.288-9.

ferent implications and needs to be addressed in different ways. One strand is the importance of the patterns and forms of worship not being determined purely at the local level. Another is the place patterns of prayer have in maintaining the unity of the church in confessing the Christian faith.

More deeply Common Prayer can refer to the way prayers and forms of worship become part of the common memory of the people of God. This cannot be contrived or hurried. Popular religion in this sense is difficult to manipulate and springs from deep perceptions of authentic religion. The experience of the chaplains in the First World War[1] suggests that some loss of this sort of Common Prayer has a long history. If *Patterns* is used by the clergy to impose without consultation a regime of continuous change it will undermine this sort of Common Prayer. If it allows the emergence of patterns of worship that take seriously the feelings of ordinary people in parishes it is likely to encourage it.

Patterns also recognizes that the Common Prayer can be used as a synonym for Anglicanism. The belief that the whole Anglican Communion can find its unity in one liturgical form is obviously nonsense.[2] This is not to deny that there are characteristically Anglican approaches to worship; here the Introduction to *Patterns* has its own suggestions to make. It is highly unlikely that worship can be long divorced from consideration of an Anglican approach to Doctrine—see Appendix 2.

In England liturgical uniformity, like cultural uniformity, is an impossible goal for the present and has been gone for at least a century. *Patterns* seems more realistic when it says,

> 'Rather, 'common prayer' exists in the Church of England in the sense of recognizing, as one does when visiting other members of the same family, some common features, some shared experiences, language and patterns or traditions. To accept a variety of forms, dictated by local culture, is part of our Anglican heritage . . .'

2. The future

If *Patterns* is accepted by Synod what impact will it have on the shape of Church of England worship? Guessing the future is obviously a dangerous exercise. The acceptance of *Patterns* would give recogntion to 'another strand of Anglican worship'. It is difficult to predict whether the different strands would interact, coalesce or remain distinct. W. H. Frere's influential insight in 1912 that liturgical reform in England would require 'a long period of authorized experiment' before church would be in a position to form 'instructed judgments' seems correct.[3]

[1] See above p.6.
[2] Developing treatment of this issue can be traced in R. C. D. Jasper *Development.* It has reached its latest stage with the establishment of biannual Anglican Liturgical Consultations. The 1989 Consultation at York produced a major statement on inculturation, David Holeton (ed.) *Findings of the Third International Anglican Kiturgical Consultation* (Grove Brooks, Bramcote, 1989), pp.3-7.
[3] R. C. D. Jasper, pp.86-87.

4. NEW TEXTS

by Trevor Lloyd

Almost certainly no other official English liturgical textbook since 1552 contains so much new writing. Gone are the days when liturgical scholars could be regarded as archaeologists translating and re-arranging ancient liturgical texts. Inevitably, as with any other similar production, there is a lot of borrowing and amending from other sources—some of it is noted below—but there is also some fresh new writing and new uses of scriptural texts. And it is not always easy to tell which is new and which is amended. There are at least two reasons for this.

Typography and participation

First, the typographical layout of *Patterns* (apart, oddly, from the introductions to confession) puts every item, irrespective of its origins, into sense-equivalent lines. This was a principle strongly advocated by the late Geoffrey Cuming, originally used in the preparation for the ASB only for the eucharistic prayers and later extended haphazardly to other parts of that book. The results are almost the same as using speech-equivalent lines, and make the text easier to say as well as easier to understand, as the breaks in thought become clearer.

This practice has been followed not just for parts said by the whole congregation, but for all the spoken material: those leading worship (particularly lay people leading sometimes unfamiliar material) will be helped by this.

Language and concept

Second, the Commission was working with clear linguistic criteria, partly imposed by the need to produce texts easily usable with families including young people, and in inner urban areas. The criteria are reproduced as part of the commentary on page 273 of *Patterns,* and a glance at them will show that they do not indicate a move towards 'lowest common denominator' language. Indeed, the language used both by children and in UPAs is often very vivid! The style of language represents a deliberate move away from the more formal, conceptual, committee and ideas-based style of the ASB, towards something more direct and personal, using concrete, tangible, visually vivid language. The Commission had its views on this reinforced—and discovered an interesting way of testing language for visual imagery rather than non-visual concepts—at a meeting with representatives from the Council for the Deaf. As we worshipped, the difficulties of deaf-signing the theological language of the ASB eucharistic prayers were very apparrent, and contrasted clearly with the ease of signing the consistent picture and story language of one of the Commission's new eucharistic prayers.

It is interesting to reflect how looking at the needs of minorities sometimes brings us back to providing for the whole church in a more biblical way. The *Children in the Way* report encouraged us to look at worship and learning as an activity the whole family of the church engages in together—with obvious implications for language and story-content. And making our worship more vivid in this kind of way makes us use both language and methods of communication which are nearer to those of Jesus—and that is not 'simpler' or bringing the level 'down'. The juxtaposition of two vivid images, or a bit of a story, can make us ask profound questions about ourselves and our relationships, or provoke us to make links of a clearly theological nature between our experience of the world and the presence of God. Worshippers sometimes need more reflective space to do the theology themselves, rather than have liturgists and synodical factions make it explicit for them in words they do not understand.

It has clearly been easier to use vivid pictures in new writing, but the economy of style reflected in some of the other criteria—avoidance of latinate constructions, preferring the shorter word and the shorter sentence, getting the rhythm right, and using inclusive language—have had a clear effect on material taken over from elsewhere.

There is insufficient space for a detailed source-criticism of the new book, but the section-by-section comments that follow attempt to bring out some of the issues involved in using both old and new material. Where items are said to be by 'the Commission', that by no means implies sixteen people sitting round a table, each contributing a line or phrase when their turn comes round. Most such items are largely the work of one member, occasionally two, subsequently improved by a group of the Commission, or by the whole Commission, and agreed by the whole Commission as representing its mind. It is because of this process of improvement and agreement that the individual member would rarely wish to claim an item as 'mine'. Numbers in brackets refer to paragraphs within the relevant Resource Section of *Patterns.*

Introduction

Discussion of the 'Examples of Home-made introductions' in the Chelmsford report, *For the Family* (1987), led to the provision of some Introductions which are prayers, one taken direct from the Chelmsford report (7), another (5) re-written from this Chelmsford prayer: 'Lord, teach us to pray, Lord, keep our thoughts from wandering. Help us to worship you in Spirit and in truth; through . . .' Some of the responsive prayer introductions come from elsewhere—(1) from Canada, (3) from New Zealand—but the statements of where we stand as we begin worship are entirely new (6, 8, 9, 13).

Confessions

The idea of providing alternative seasonal and thematic invitations to confession (allowed for in the ASB) is not new. There are some good examples in David Silk's *In Penitence and Faith* (Mowbray, 1988) though only two (Easter and Kingdom) are directly copied here. Similarly, the idea of providing sentences between the petitions of the Kyrie is not new, being found in the Roman Missal, David Silk's booklet above, and in the Commission's earlier *Lent, Holy Week, Easter* (1986, p.286). What is new in these examples is keeping to one theme and developing it, and also the suggestion that, with suitably penitential insertions, such material might *occasionally* replace the normal confession. This latter provision might well be seen by the Synod as potentially too divisive: the form of the confession has in the past been one of the more difficult things for Synod to agree on, and if this proposal was seen as enabling a kyrie pattern to be used as the only form of confession in some churches it would rightly be regarded as an impoverishment and not an enrichment of the liturgy.

Some of the confessions themselves are completely new writing, like those based on one chapter of scripture (*4* 2.2; *8* 2.5; *15* 2.8; *16* 2.9), or the one used in the sample baptism service (*17* 2.13). These demonstrate the value of occasionally departing from a well-known omnibus confession of the traditional type, to use a confession which explores penitentially one scriptural theme.

One or two of the responsive confessions (*6* 2.4, *9* 2.6, *12* 2.7, *17* 2.10) originate from *Church Family Wroship* (Hodder and Stoughton, 1986). A comparison of the Creation confession with that at section 511 in *Church Family Worship* shows a change in wording which raises an issue for those who write such material, including those who write hymns and songs. Sometimes the sentiments expressed are too specific and personal for everyone to be able to say, 'Yes, that's me' with integrity, and liturgists and song-writers are guilty of forcing people to say something they do not feel is true. One way of overcoming this is to employ the 'When we are bad, forgive us' style: so, in *Church Family Worship* 511 we have 'When we enjoy the fruits of the harvest, but forget they come from you . . .'. The Commission clearly felt that the confession of sin involved a clear statement of fact, rather than a phrase which could be construed as a future possibility or even (if the 'when' were taken to mean 'whenever') a request for continuing forgiveness the next time and the next . . . So *Patterns* goes for

'We enjoy the fruits of the harvest,
but sometimes forget . . .'.

The next petition in the original is 'When we are full and satisfied, but ignore the cry of the hungry and those in need . . .', and *Patterns* neatly avoids the peril of declaring that everyone in the congregation is full, with

'We belong to a people who are full and satisfied,
but ignore the cry of the hungry.'

On the next petition ('When we are thoughtless, and do not treat with respect or care the wonderful world you have made') *Patterns* is persuaded that pretty well everyone can acknowledge being thoughtless and abbreviates (the tightening of the language is typical of the changes made) to

'We are thoughtless
and do not care enough for the world you have made'.

And in the last petition ('When we store up good for ourselves alone' in the original), *Patterns* has us looking round at our neighbours with

'Some of us store up goods for ourselves alone'!

An interesting—and typical—set of issues arising from amending other people's work . . .

Three of the confessions are ancient material re-worked: two sensitive you-form versions of the Book of Common Prayer confessions drafted by one member of the Commission with outside advice, and a modern version of the 'Man, born of woman' from the funeral service, made responsive by the inclusion of the tris-hagion. A slightly different version of the latter will be found in the Advent chapter of the Commission's subsequent publication, *The Promise of His Glory.*

Apart from the last three, the confessions have specific absolutions attached to them, some of the new writing, others from the Scottish 1982 Liturgy (*6* 2.4), St. Augustine (*9* 2.6), Dean Colet (*17* 2.10), the American Presbyterian *Daily Prayer, Supplement Liturgical Resource 5* (*17* 2.12), and *Lent, Holy Week, Easter* (*17* 2.11).

Affirmations of Faith

There are two sorts of material here. First, there are credal excerpts from scripture, largely from the NIV, originally reproduced in *Church Family Worship:* Philippians 2, 1 Corinthians 15 and Revelation 4 and 5. Because they are scripture, they clearly have some authority, and could be equally recited as canticle or praise material. The Commission looked at some of the other alternative credal materials available, but felt that most were too far away from either scripture or the agreed statements of faith in the church to bear the weight of this kind of use. The Commission was tempted to include one or two credal hymns, but found nothing close enough to a traditional form of creed: one has now been commissioned and written, and might be suitable for inclusion here at a later date. The debate here will centre on whether the Commission, by admitting a small number of texts of absolute validity and carefully labelling them 'Affirmations of Faith' and not 'Creeds', has opened the floodgates to a mass of divisive and undesirable material which will lead the church doctrinally astray, or whether the Commisson, by being so timid and apparently legalistic, has closed its eyes to what is actually going on in growing churches which use a variety of songs and choral spoken material at this point.

Second, there are new ways of presenting credal material which is already authorized: a very effective responsive version of the Nicene Creed, the short baptismal creed (amended for inclusive language) the longer interrogative from the Apostles' Creed which appeared in *Lent, Holy Week, Easter,* and, most interestingly, an attempt to revive the Athanasian Creed by including a section of it in a new translation, in responsive form, as an affirmation of incarnational faith.

Prayer

There are some things in the *Notes* to this section which are familiar, the alternative introductions to the Lord's Prayer, largely from the Roman *Divine Office,* and the suggestions for weightier endings to the ASB Rite A intercessions, from Michael Vasey's Grove Booklet *Intercessions in the Eucharist* (Grove Booklet, 1982), but the most significant is the attempt to introduce some standard forms for litany-style intercessions. Often litanies fail because people do not know where to come in with the response, unless they have their eyes open to a full text in front of them. Here we have some standard responses, each with its own recognizably different trigger words, accompanied by two addtional alternatives to provide some welcome variety to the now standard ASB Rite A intercession ending 'Merciful Father . . . '. Even if only a few of these catch on, or are deliberately learnt, it may help congregations to pray without having to follow a full text of the intercessions. And the assumption that this is likely to happen has been made in the intercessions in three of the six *Sample Cards* already published (GS Misc. 328, 1989).

Much of the new writing by the Commission for the responsive prayers is marked by standing much closure to scripture than is normal for this kind of material: see, for example *2* 5.4, *6* 5.6 and *15* 5.15. And there are other prayers on the pattern 'Lord, in the Gospel you did this . . . [scripture reference]; now therefore act in this current situation [description]' the Commission's Family intercession at *13* 5.13 is an example of this.

Another interesting example of the amendment of material from other sources may be seen in the intercession for the church (*11* 5.12, based on section 477 in *Church Family Worship*). Some of the proposals for change in this prayer were raised by a group at a Commission consultation for diocesan liturgical committee secretaries, some by the group responsible for the report *Called to be adult disciples* (GS 794). As a result, the 'bless those who . . . yet . . .' pattern of the original has been abandoned as sometimes forcing an unreal contrast, and the last two sections added in order to underline two facts: first, in praying for the church we pray not only for those who minister in 'churchy' ways within the body, but for those who are still part of the body in their daily working lives; and second, life for the Christian is not always a triumph, nor decisions clear-cut, so we pray about complexity and powerlessness. This is just one of the many instances of the Commission having its eyes on the inner city.

The section of post-communion prayers and prayer endings for word services includes little that is absolutely new, but very many instances of wholesale revision of prayers from the Westcott House office book, the Missal, the prayer books of the Anglican churches in Canada, Australia and New Zealand and other places and individuals. One example of such changes is *1* 52,3, where the Westcott House original ('Almighty God, grant that as your Son Jesus Christ has come to us in this bread and this cup, so we may be preserved . . .') becomes

> 'Loving Father, your Son Jesus Christ has come to us
> in word and Spirit, in bread and cup.
> Preserve us . . .'.

Praise

The Praise section of *Patterns,* the longest in the book, contains a vast amount of material, almost all based on scripture, which can be used as accalamations and responses, responsive psalm-like pieces which can be used responsively or as a canticle, as well as new songs (the *Patterns* term for canticles) and eucharistic prefaces and thanksgivings. Much of this material is entirely new: in the nine pieces for Resurrection, Trinity and Spirit, for instance, only one has appeared in another book. There are enough items here on the theme of light to brighten the gloom of half a dozen evening offices, and others on flowing water, saints, dying and creation with obvious uses. Some of these would do well as the doxological climax to a service of the word, some of them end with the sanctus, and some have been specially tailored to become a eucharistic thanksgiving for use with the new Eucharistic Prayer D. Some of the longer scriptural pieces in the latter might well do with optional omissions built into them to reduce the overall length, but one at least is easily useable with children: most of it could even be made to fit the tune 'Jesus is a friend of mine', with the responses changed . . .

Though some of the twenty-five new canticles which complete this section are derived from the SSF Office Book, the Canadian Book of Alternative Services, and the New Zealand Prayer Book, most have been so thoroughly revised that it is hard to tell which was the original text. The Commission had the draft of the Revised English Bible before them, and some of the inclusive language suggestions in particular come from there. Each canticle has an optional response provided, and is not as yet pointed. The only non-scriptural canticle is the delightful 'Song of Anselm' which appeared in *Making Woman Visible* (CHP, 1989).

Introductory Words

All but four of the twenty-seven new introductory words of the Peace are new, including ones for use at weddings and funerals. The introductory note gives some encouragement for the pattern to be copied. There is more new writing in the paragraphs for dedicating gifts and people, which may be at the offertory, or earlier in the service. This section also includes some new words, noteably some reflecting the Didache, for use at the breaking of bread.

Eucharistic Prayers

A fuller comment on the origins of these prayers is in GS Misc 333 (5). The five main differences from the ASB prayers are deliberate and noteworthy. First, there is only one epiclesis, or invocation of the Spirit, and it comes (in highly variable form!) some time after the narrative of institution. Second, the credal pattern for the long preface or thanksgiving, itemizing in some form the mighty works of God, has been abandoned in favour of a more variable approach. This could have its dangers, as mention of the resurrection would appear to be optional in the last two prayers, but then there is a very clear focus on the cross in all four which seems entirely in line with scripture which also fails to mention the resurrection event in connection with the supper. Third, the words of the narrative are variable, and fit closely with the style of each prayer. To insist on having the same words each time is to exalt those words to a position of importance they should not have, unless we believe they have some effect by being those particular words . . . There may be those who would prefer the narrative always to refer to the bread and wine in a 'this is . . .' formula, and this could easily be amended if the whole church felt it necessary. Fourth, the position of the sanctus is variable, coming virtually at the end, in the climactic position in prayers A and C, and in a 'Rite A' position between the preface and the narrative in B and D. Fifth, all the prayers are highly responsive, indicating clearly that the celebration is one of president and people together.

This responsive element is tackled differently in each prayer. In Prayer A, apart from the traditional dialogue and sanctus, there are three responsive elements: two long-ish passages from Revelation, responding first to creation and then to redemption (people will need the text for these, unless they are sung); the Roman offertory response in the creation section, a bold attempt to indicate that what is done with bread and wine in relation to God is a proper part of the thanksgiving; and congregational words for the taking of the bread and wine, part of the epiclesis, and the breaking of bread, which also includes an anamnetic element. Here the president is the orchestrator of a priestly action, some of which is clearly in the mouths if not the hands of the people.

On the face of it, Prayer B, much revised from its Roman Catholic original draft (and the only one of the four prayers to have a source outside the Commission), looks much more like the standard 'Rite A' pattern as far as the responses go, and the main interest centres, probably rightly, on the evocative language and on the innovation (not in the original) of three variable insertions which seasonally and thematically change the character of the prayer. But if the little note allowing the repetition at intervals of one line—'to you be glory and praise for ever!'—the whole thing becomes a majestic burst of congregational praise.

The responses in Prayer C are varied—the congregation will need it in front of them until they have learnt it—and denote the Trinitarian structural movement of the prayer, with addresses in succession to Father, Son (three times) and Spirit. And in the non-variable part of Prayer D the responses are on the 'Rite A' pattern again: as with Prayer B without the one-line acclamation, no text is needed for the congregation. But with its interesting provision for variable long prefaces drawn from the thanksgivings earlier in the book, some of the suggested standard praise responses will be in use with this prayer. This is the least innovative of the four prayers, despite this provision and its extreme shortness: in its first draft the anamnesis-epiclesis was in fact a line shorter but the Commission were not deliberately trying to break records, only responding to the many requests for some shorter eucharistic prayers.

Blessings

The Commission remains innovative to the end, with a selection of new blessings, some (like ones amended from Australia, Ireland and New Zealand) in the traditional form, some highly responsive ones, and some modelled on the Roman tripartite form. But here the language is tighter than the Missal, and the thought develops from one part to the next, moving from scripture to experience.

5. LEARNING TO WORSHIP

by Trevor Lloyd

The publication, the continuing debate about, and the bringing into use of, these new *Patterns for Worship* is an educational exercise for the whole church—and seen as such by the compilers. It may well be that at one level the Church will learn through this more of what it wants from any successor—or family of successors—to the ASB after the year 2000. It may enable those who want something free-er than the ASB to talk to those who want to close down the options and return to a more traditional way of doing liturgy: it may even help to show the possibilities of a mixture of ancient and modern. But at local level new liturgy should promote learning about God, and about how he is to be worshipped.

The introduction to the Commentary at the end of *Patterns* recognizes the need for a relationship between doing worship and learning about it:

> 'Worship is not worship until you do it.
> It is no longer sufficient in the Church of England to produce a worship book which consists simply of texts to say or sing. That is a bit like producing a recipe which is a list of ingredients without the instructions for putting them together'.

It is well known that the present Commission has been looking at questions of liturgical formation—the way Christians are 'formed' or helped to grow as Christians both through the liturgy and by a deeper understanding of it. Worship involves encouraging people in esperiential learning about God, about themselves as they are given space to reflect on and measure up to his word and presence, and about the society they live in. Worship involves doing some theology—it is not just the result of someone else having done some theology, but an active engagement with the nature and word of God. Worship involves doing theology ecclesiologically, in the context of the society of the church set in the midst of a wider society: it is not something to be done solo, but in relationship with others and with an eye to its effect on the whole church. And worship involves doing theology not only ecclesiologically but ultimately doxologically: what is done in worship is not done in a study with texts, nor in a debate about theology and doctrinal correctness, but in bringing praise and glory to God, exalting him to his rightful place in our lives and in society.

It is not just a matter of everything being connected to everything else, but the praise of God being the driving force behind the connections. Liturgical formation is about helping people to make and use the links, in order 'to praise God not only with our lips but in our lives'. And this book contributes to the development of liturgical formation in two main ways, overtly and by implication.

Formation and instruction

The overt contribution of this book to liturgical formation is the wide range of different ways in which educational material, hints and tips on preparation and presentation are brought before the reader. In the *Introduction* there is, for instance, some discussion of 'Family' Services which will help those entering this field, or reviewing their situation, and also a list of reasons why reading the bible in church often does not work, with some pointers to how to improve the situation. This again could well be used for example by those in a training or discussion session for lesson readers. And it would help if more people in our churches, and not only those who lead, had some understanding of how the different parts of a service relate to one another. The sections in the *Introduction* on Structure and on the Eucharistic Prayers would help here, and the *Instructions* for the Service of the Word and for the Eucharist do a similar job, but in greater detail and with diagrams. They contain a blow-by-blow account of how to put a service together, the choices to be made, and some examples.

The *Instructions* vary from practical detail, sometimes designed to move the church on from what might have occupied its attention in the past (such as instructions for the ablutions—'This is not a significant liturgical act and need not be done at the holy table or by the president') to helping people to see the 'deep structures' of the Eucharistic prayer. Though there is a very full menu given for the Eucharistic Prayer, there is, of course, no hint that the constructing of such a prayer might be done locally! But it would clearly help if worship leaders had more knowledge of how the prayer is constructed: it might help them not to use a more 'holy' tone of voice at one point, ot not to encourage the congregation to drop to their knees half way through what is supposed to be one prayer.

This section also contains ten *Guidelines,* a set of questions to ask about each service as it is planned. These cover a wide range of different areas, and could each be the subject of discussion and policy decisions by the group responsible for worship. For example, 'Is music used in such a way as to further and develop the main thrust of the service? Is there too much musical praise, with two many choir items, or too long a section of choruses from the band, or hymns too close to one another?' And the last one forces people to look at the ecclesial character of what is done: 'check that the contents are not divisive, and can be used by children, single people, the bereaved, members of broken families'.

The next main area of instruction (for those who skip all the introductory material?) is contained in the introductory paragraphs and notes at the beginning of every *Resource Section.* These are a combination of three things. There are practical suggestions ('Well-prepared notices, including some announcement of the day's themes, can serve to unite a congregation as a family . . .'). There are references to the rubrics of Rite A, showing how most of what is suggested already falls within what is allowed there, and encouraging worship leaders to use a little imagination ('Some ways of varying this greeting are indicated below'). And there are occasional pushes at the Rite A boundaries, sometimes with reference to the provisions of the *Outline Services.* Some of these paragraphs, such as those on the Kyrie and on Blessings, give some help to those who want to write their own prayers.

At the end of the book comes the *Commentary*—sample sections only because of the novelty of its form. Believing (like the Doctrine Commission report, *Believing in the Church*), in the importance of story as a unitive educational medium—see the section on reading the bible in the *Introduction* for a fuller argument—the Commission has developed a story-telling commentary. This focuses on four churches—St. Andrew's, which has something of the feel of a suburban mildly charismatic church in a newish building; St. Bartholomew's, a collection of country villages with medieval buildings; St. Christopher's, which looks like a forward-looking inner urban 'catholic' tradition; and St. David's, which might also have been labelled St. Dumdum's or St. Dodo's: D stands for disaster and those at St. David's get everything wrong. And in with the stories, usually on the opposite page, are little boxes full of lists of options, things to consider, draft service plans, etc. It will help if in a subsequent commercial edition these are properly laid out with coloured panels, and arrows or something to integrate them more closely with the stories. The idea is that when the PCC or the worship group want to look at a particular area of worship, like re-arranging the furniture, planning the service, or how to use the creed or lead the intercessions, the group reads the four stories, sees if it identifies with any of them, and is provoked into a discussion which will end up with some useful proposals. It may, of course, have more fun writing a yet more entertaining version of St. David's from its own experience . . .

At first glance, *Patterns for Worship* may look too complicated for children and for UPAs. This view does not only belittle the intelligence, adaptability and different ways of working of these two groups in particular, but also reveals a misunderstanding of the nature of the book. It is not a service book, to be taken and used as such—even the large section of *Sample Services,* though available to be used 'off the peg' is mainly there as part of the instructional material, to demonstrate how the new 'patterns' can be made to work. Rather, *Patterns* is a book for those who prepare worship—and the hint is heavily given that this should not be the vicar on his own but a group with differing gifts, working, learning and growing together in this ministry. What really matters is that the services which are the outcome of it at local level should be easy to get hold of and find your way through.

Formation and Growing

One thing is clear: though the instructional and formation material is deliberately spread through the different areas of the book, the overall message is a unitive one. The whole production points in the same direction. But it is true that this way of planning and producing worship demands much more from those who lead and prepare, and that even those recently trained in theological colleges may not have the liturgical experience necessary. The book, in that light, is a dangerous one. Worship will deteriorate in quality if a book like this is simply picked up and used without much thought. What is needed, as well as groups using the educational material incorporated in the book, is a series of workshops and conferences at different levels run by diocesan liturgical committees and diocesan adult education officers, for both clergy and lay worship